CITIES AT DAWN

CITIES
AT
DAWN

GEOFFREY NUTTER

WAVE BOOKS

SEATTLE & NEW YORK

Published by Wave Books

www.wavepoetry.com

Copyright © 2016 by Geoffrey Nutter

All rights reserved

Wave Books titles are distributed to the trade by

Consortium Book Sales and Distribution

Phone: 800-283-3572 / SAN 631-760X

Library of Congress Cataloging-in-Publication Data

Names: Nutter, Geoffrey, 1968– author.

Title: Cities at dawn / Geoffrey Nutter.

Description: First edition. | Seattle : Wave Books, [2016]

Identifiers: LCCN 2015047527| ISBN 9781940696331

(limited edition hardcover)

| ISBN 9781940696324 (softcover)

Classification: LCC PS3614.U88 A6 2016 | DDC 811/.6—dc23

LC record available at http://lccn.loc.gov/2015047527

Designed and composed by Quemadura

Printed in the United States of America

9 8 7 6 5 4 3 2 1

First Edition

Wave Books 060

to Elaine Nutter-Diaz and Samuel Nutter-Diaz

CITIES
AT
DAWN

A SMALL VICTORIAN OBJECT

Here is a purely functional object:
remote-controlled substation no. 10,
a utilitarian structure down by the tracks
that run past the ruined marina.
It was built in 1931 and is now being renovated.
Scaffolding has been erected all along its sides.
A big coil of damp rope
is lying in a pile of broken
concrete, brick, and plaster.
The topmost row of the chain-link fence
that runs along the river is twisted
into barbs, and shredded plastic sacks
are snagged in the barbs as far as the eye can see:
dirty gray and shredded, flapping in the wind.
A candy box, once green, has been
bleached out to light blue by the sun.
Silent gray boulders are lapped at by waves.
Signs are posted to warn against
the consumption of eels by children.
What's that in the mud where the tide is going out?

———

Buttons; bottle caps; small bits of Styrofoam
that look like shells or coral; a few dead crabs;
a cracked porcelain vessel from the Victorian era
for containing the tears shed by those
who have survived the death of loved ones.

CLASS E ORDINARY OPEN
HIGH-SIDED WAGON

Just past the cake shop at the edge of town
we came across the railroad bridge,
and watched the gray freight car
pass under us and under the ice-covered trestles.
It is filled with rusted pieces of machinery,
with slate and ballast, unwashed gravel,
foundry sand, fragments, green, of bottle-glass.
Where is it going with them?
Will they rebuild something on the far
horizon of the snows, the rusted-metal
golem of the snows? And as the choir
of the landscape sings about the beauty
of the land with the land's voice,
and the beauty of the bare and shredded trees,
the freight car passes us, passes bridges,
headed toward the sun. The freight car
is filled with bent rebar, rusted
hundredweight bevel gears and huge
steel springs, with radiator grillwork

---

and hair-like clumps of wire caked
with chunks of concrete. And what stealth
conceals its ultimate intentions?
It is headed north, toward the North Pole,
toward the towering Maypole where
a crucible of ingenuity will burn off
all impurities in the purest sun.
But first it must pass through Nebraska.

THE LAPIDARY CRYSTAL

Entering beleaguered cities
at night by port or by air: if by air
on landing strips just beyond
the ribbon roads, and if by port
through public markets and their
vendors of finger jade, then down
steep stairs that lead to Cat Street
past the Tea Library, through
alleyways and barbershops
with names like Toy Apple Beauty.
And its citizens are sleeping
but many are awake, and those
who are awake are turning in their beds,
as others lay their heads upon the cold
night pillows stuffed with ash and jasmine
for the calming of insomniacs;
others are burning the midnight oil
with a white and incandescent flame,
boiling a melon in a bath of caustic potash,
or incubating blue eggs, nodding off

———

in senate chambers under red-gold
portraits of past governors;
in the stone and glass pavilion
of the orthopedic surgeons
or the porn-strewn bamboo forests
that grow beside the highway
they are consulting maps and ancient books,
reading the illuminated tablets
or examining the facets of the blue
many-faceted stone. Others
are dining long past midnight,
on smoked eel and lemongrass
on square green plates; they
are smoking hookahs, drinking brilliant
red drinks and lighting Roman candles,
or preparing perfumes from extract
of geranium or oil of rose and vetiver.
And in the subterranean food court
with its huge Walpolian hand for signage
lit with burning fustian, purple bulbs,
and treacle, they are eating tentacles
in man-made noodles, and motherhood
is ripening. And when dawn comes

and the city starts to shine,
some of its buildings rude and unfinished,
some giant white beehives, eggs, or open domes
shooting showers of sparks into the air—
two men lie full-length beside the river,
asleep in their pointed boots in the tall weeds
in the lee of a moss-covered boulder.
A few instructional pamphlets
are scattered in the dirt beside them:
one on how to flavor cigars; the other
on the annealing of bronze for bells;
the last on the shining of the lapidary crystal.

BILLET-DOUX

A green cube on the varnished tabletop, a gourd
beside it. And next to that an ashtray made from fired
    clay
that some child made in school for Mother's Day.
The Tomboy drummed her fingers on the tabletop,
a sheet of loose-leaf, violet, in front of her.
She had drawn, in green ink, a part of one scene
of one summer day in August, when she had found
a large bed of sea flowers at the very edge of the tide,
their violet faces lifted just above the sand
beneath the overcast sky. It was strange to see these
    flowers
on the sand so near the sea—she had wanted to touch
    them.
They belonged among the group of simple beings,
the one that included her. This sheet of grape-colored
paper, this is where she brainstormed the secretest
billet-doux that ever would be left unwritten by a girl
of twelve who would never grow older.
The yellow gourd drifted across the table toward her.

———

THE MAN WHO WAS USED UP

My father was wounded in the Great War.
He lost his face in a fierce battle,
a flanking maneuver, a counterattack,
a mission of "forlorn hope." But which Great
War? One of many wars. One of many
Giant Wars. One ordinary titan war.

And my father kept a glass cabinet
of wax noses in his study, and changed
his nose several times a day. He had
lost an eye in an offensive, a night
operation, a minor skirmish, one
of many small loose parts that are pulled
together and called "The Great War."

Now he had a glass eye. One eye was glass
and the other was pewter—though the pewter
eye had been his eye before the war, before
the bayonet charge, the reckoning barrage.
These are among the things he carried:

---

a steel jaw, a diamond tooth, a prosthetic
limb (an arm, to be precise),
a hook for a hand. And he kept his eye,
his tooth, a hook, a pair of pinking shears,
and the rubberized semblance of a hand
in a wooden case with small compartments
like a box of chocolates from the country
where he had fought amid the dikes
and earthworks, during the land war,
the one between the sea war and the sky war.

And he had children, too, besides me. There
were children, legitimate children, and two
or three false children; there were bastards,
doppelgängers, changelings. There was
a wax child, and a glass child, and a fire child
(though that last was not a child at all
but merely a fire with which he lit his pipe).
And he had a mandrake root, a mandragora,
a suit of armor made of bone. And we
who consisted yet of all our original parts,
were strangers to you, or so it seemed.

You had a gun kept on the wall near the head
of a deer bearing very large antlers.
And we were there crouching down in the flower beds,
watching you remove your flowered shirt.
And we stood tall among the presences.

THESE GREAT SENTINELS

These great sentinels
have been here so much longer than you,
bare as January, January bees,
bare as rain or boats of commerce snarled
on the highly trafficked waterway,
as the bowsprit of the Dutch fishing pink
(one of many curious boats)
or the Malay rigging of the Bombay yacht
(another one of many curious boats)
and the lights along the turrets of the cliffs
along the harbor basin shined.

And Mrs. Hannah Glasse set her cliffside house
in order—it was a house of glass—
as if to tell you that all people
in glass houses should be glass people,
half made of rain, who watch the levitating stone
with rising unease, the way one dreams uneasily.

Something, it seems,
has tamed us: and the living hand
opens in its giving gesture.
And out above the water burst
the Roman candles of July,
the apple-green Meistersingers,
the long fire of an open secret, aquatic trees,
the blue chrysanthemums of Jupiter, of love.

And these great sentinels have torn
a page of strange remembrance
from your endless calendar
to let the cool wind charm you
(the cool wind of July—for a fragrance
of jasmine drifted over from the palace, from the forest).
For each season has its delights,
as each key unlocks a door—but the key
does not tell you which door it opens,
nor in which building, however transparent,
you will find it.

CANALS PANELED WITH LIGHT

Shy one, and sweet: don't worry—
it's time we were getting to bed.
You who rode the train down into the city
and stood beneath the orange building
with "Mr. Tang" in flashing letters
eight yards high; who bore the tidings
of home along through foreignness,
ogled by a man who wore a coat
and tie woven from strange purple weaves,
a glinting fabric that seemed
to be covered with blinking eyes,
or staring eyes, all of which
were staring at you also, for a moment.
And all I've been doing all day
is sitting on the ocean's manifold hay,
which is stacked up
into breakers eight yards high that break
upon the cypresses and panel the canal
with light. It differs, in a thousand ways,
with itself, as you do, sweet, and I.

───────

But the bringing time draws near,
whatever, and whenever, that might be.
And you sail home past Flushing Meadows,
past the black Stop signs
and brazil-nut-colored thumbprint
over the smokestack and the watchtower,
the canceled séance and the sunset.
And the canceled sea and the sunset
panel the canal with light.

THE RADIANT MANIFEST

Amid pagodas, kiosks, and statues,
the center place of great interests is the Winding
Lily Pond. There are not only the artificial lotus
but also plenty of tiny structures built into the waterless
    pond.
A few yards from here one will be amused by a thrilling
    scene:
A long and big python with raising head and out-shot
    tongue.
And a pond full of models of different aquatic spirits.
And the sun shines down upon all with its own version
of truthfulness—one not so much of verifiable fact—
but a prodigy of being for all that. Golden bees
seem to have awakened in the tree beside you.
I too had greeted the probabilities, the double-sided
panels that turn toward one another, then away
at intervals, depending on the speed and direction of the
    wind.
And we were attempting to "think it through" in the
    way that we knew how.

But it's not something you can think your way through—
You think your way in and stay there.

Nevertheless, the garden has manifested a great calm
    (its great calm),
the calm of the man for whom its thoughts become his
    own.
Then you start to hear even the faraway noise of the sea.
Once, enchantment seized me when I heard it, and the
    tears
I was brought to were shed in the usual mode of such
    shedding:
silver, flecked with gems, suffusing everything around me,
and the shops selling terra-cotta storage jars, parsley pots,
insect-repellent garden candles, umbrella stands,
weather vanes and aromatic oils, oblong willow trugs,
wallpapers velvet and damask, as well as jellied eels and
    antique clocks,
seemed such common haunted places, there seemed to
    be no obstacle
between them and whatever had possessed me,
all being strangers beyond concealment,
as if all flamed in glass and only saw completion

there amid the graces shifting in a pattern.
These too were interpolations, as the small six-eaved
    bridges
crossing over to where the plants were spreading
their gentle arms, and the hyacinth, fire-eyed,
like something born only at break of day.

THESE ARE THE CLIFFS OF WONDER

When we moved from the wilderness
(of our feelings), past the granite quarry
and the saltworks and the winding
towers (of our feelings), through
the coal gas plants and gravel-crushing
structures and blast furnaces
and limekilns (of our feelings),
to the far, rotting bridges (of our feelings),
and thence to the suburbs
(of our feelings), there too the dark
eucalyptus trees lined avenues
where the lone eye in the cubit stone
was venerating Makepeace Thackeray.
And here is the half-frozen snow
of centuries of meditation.

Now the snow is brittle.
The river doves are flying
from the river that is coming
through the town. The river is frozen

under the bridges. The houses
stand along the town. In the
town and along its borders,
the wind is blowing, and
blowing against the rockface
of the quarries.

These are the Cliffs of Wonder.
They rise from the Sea of Astonishment,
gray and solid there beneath
the Sky of Accelerating Clouds
of Years. The Person of Day-to-Day
Living lived, day in, day out, among
the Big Geraniums of Guesses and the Waves,
in the Shadow of the Rickety
Lighthouse of Conjecturing.
What is he holding in his Hands?
A Ball of Crystal. A Raindrop.
A Beam of Light is sweeping
over the Waters.

THE MERCURIAL WHEEL

One type of perpetual motion machine
is the mercurial wheel. Below two turning pivots,
water flows into a cistern, where it shimmers,
clear and still, but the series
of bevels and spirals keep turning.
This machine, however, is imaginary.
It works very well in the realm
where the red flower of opium is carved
in stone or jet above the gatehouse,
a harbinger, perhaps for argonauts,
of things to come. Do you think
scalding emeralds count as money
in that town? That could be.
But more than likely friends and friends of friends
will see them flowing down a channel,
past a birdbath overflowing with green
and moss-covered water in the overgrown grass,
past Garibaldi, bearded on his plinth
of marble. Does he sheathe or unsheathe

the curving saber? It is both, and neither.
And as the melody coming from the music box
is only a suggestion, it too is mercurial,
with no discernible use. Now let us read
a poem.

THE DOOR INTO SUMMER

You threw back the covers of your bed
and there was the cat, surprised awake,
the cat that was pretending to be you,
the cat that had kittened in the night.
There were octuplets, eight small
trembling sea roses, small, rose-colored.
The mother cat is carefully licking her white paw,
then drawing the paw across her face.
I'm just going to look at them awhile,
okay? If you'll permit me. The sun
is coming up. That was one day.

On another day, two small people,
among the small talk, perhaps the very
smallest possible talk, as insignificant
as bluish flowerets or tea, began to fall in love.
But no one saw them. And they
were of little consequence, or almost
none at all. But I saw them.
This is not wish fulfillment.

———

These are not the pleasurings of enmity,
fulfillments in the world that lets a child
die before its parents. Only children
can forget themselves just long enough
to fall in love. Then, at the height of day,
having left their crumpled houses
blue among geraniums and well
within earshot of the sea and the bells,
they return to the world separately,
bringing back no stratagem
save the abandonment of stratagem that is love.
Later, when the marriage knot is tangled
they will sit together, winding the spool:
just two simple people on a summer day.

PORTRAIT

This is a portrait of my father the soldier:
the onetime vendor of cabbage-nets,
onetime carpenter, gardener, repairer of pistons,
erstwhile angler twisting wire and feather
into lures with pliers; onetime plasterer,
amateur surveyor, onetime dealer of dogs,
mariner, supposed pilot of amphibious vehicles;
clockmaker—look into his eyes: shy gray eyes
like the osprey or the plover, shy eyes
that seem ashamed of the weapon he carried—
it was something to be utilized, one more
among the tools of tradesmen, one
more conveyer of heat and energy,
the blade like a saber, not a saber,
but a blade-like sword of grass
plucked from a tuft of summer vegetation,
wielded by the hand like signals directing
the movements of cranes and hoists,
one more journeyman.

And though he killed your father, the printer,
a manufacturer of scented pocket calendars
and other printed matter before he was a soldier,
we somehow ended up together,
and in our home, above the fire,
we kept their portraits, two soldiers,
two shy young men before they were fathers.

RENÉ DESCARTES

Say the neighbor planet was the source of all rain, friend.

Rain and sanctuary; sanctuary, rain.

And just as sanctuary greened with leaves your bearings,

so the neighbor planet seemed so very near: the sanctuary
garden.

So, René Descartes: were you melancholy?

Tunneling so far distant into and away from your own
life, O Pilgrim,

O Hero, into the disquiet of a shadow life where you
might test beyond all doubt

whether this, your head, is glass, and whether those, your
arms, aren't clay,

and whether both aren't pumpkins . . . so that your
thinking might harden

into marble and you might stand in an iron glow, glowing
green

in the leaves. René Descartes, this is you laboring away
in your study.

Then to think that you can just get up and take your hat
from the peg

———

and your coat from the rack that stands like what might be
a serious man who watches you—and that you might walk
    outside
past City Hall, the statue of Erasmus in the square where
    a tree stump
is being pulled up by a system of wind-driven gears and
    pulleys;
and then down to the water where the mariners are
    tending traps,
hauling the giant red-gold bugs up from the depths.

And you can keep walking out into a field and just sit
    down
for a while. Eat your lunch on a bed of small blue flowers.
Comb your beard in a leisurely way, good man.
The steam whistle interrupts the moment's pleasures—
    but it is far away.
One might imagine that the workday has ended
at the textile mills and foundries,
and all the laborers are streaming out, on holiday.
But the industrial revolution has not happened yet.
We have more than two hundred years to sit here:
so carry on with your important work.

THE HARKENING KNELL

When I was young and brilliant
and the "harkening knell" broke nightly
from the sea, I was drugged (by sleep)
and made to follow (follow X) into the dream
of the night before. The paths there
were long, and the hours pressed apace,
their permutations were disorganized
and it seemed all friends of friends
had been replaced by changelings, and we
had fallen among the smoldering embers
of our living kindred spirits, just outside
the city that was all things to all people:
superstructures leaned above the thoroughfares;
and were we living in some fool's paradise,
and did we take apart the radio and put it back
together in reverse order, treasure up the crystal?
We searched for the perfect piece
in the scrapyard, the one on the frightening
outskirts of that giant city, piled
with scraps of sharp and twisted steel,

———

the tall yellow cranes at work picking through.
Bread was baking coolly in the moonlight,
that time we were walking over the fine
loose earth, and the powdered gypsum,
the powdered lime and the unsized stone,
and crossed the bridge over waters
flowing slowly toward the sea,
the trees on either side were black, carbonized cubes,
beleaguered; and it was fine, because we did know
that's what the Earth grows into grass with,
and we perused the lapidary manual,
its pages pressed from green grass:
When the Earth Was Young and Brilliant.

APOLOGY FOR IDLERS

All trees war against ideas.
All wood sorrel, all sea holly,
all bezique so caution, though
Rosenzweig is diamonded
and interfolded in his books,
his star. But is he standing like a man
of metal by the fences, the scent
of jasmine ice-like in the grass?
There are no ideals, save
in marl under ant-farms, the bee
in the climbing Noisette rose,
the banded hairstreak brooding
in the shade of the cold palmetto.
Some were living in a world where
fire's disciples go where they're told
without questioning. Even the boughs
of the commonest trees shine with rain
when the sun comes out, the glossy
pages of the summer book where
the yellow-streaked plums are meditating.

There is an interim of wandering, and
sunlight scatters wildly through the branches;
but then the violet clouds come gently,
tame all things. And thrushes and their allies
visit the Earth again . . . in a world of dark wars
and giants, the mysterious and mighty Earth,
patiently bearing all misunderstanding.

A PYTHIAN ODE

One day I saw a man, an old Englishman in tweeds
standing on the street, squinting into the wind, unmoving,
chin held high as his hat blew off
and tumbled, end over end, far down the street.
He was like some kind of monument—but to what?
And what if, while that figure loomed there, expecting
    to meet
my gaze, I had just turned back with a studied indifference
to the newly purchased looking-glass, cracking
macadamia nuts in an interval of silence, one more
Kidderminster Anabaptist, one more Tokyo salaryman
half asleep in a pachinko parlor,
smoking Menthol cigarettes in the middle of the day,
an eggplant smoldering on the vine,
one more who stands and waits, half nodding off,
in front of barriers the night before Black Friday.

You're resting in a cool and self-forgetful nonchalance
on a stone bench in the center of a topiary maze.
And you might slip into a kind of trance. And you

might begin to feel like a boy, just drifting down a river
in a catamaran simple as a lily under stars, blowing
tobacco smoke into the air and talking to a friend . . .
forever.

For this life is lived in fragments, made of fragments,
remembered in fragments—even before they bring down
the retributory cudgel to smash the thing that you have
    made.
One would hope that, all things being equal, one would
at least stanch the deeds that don't matter but hurt,
the pungent ones, full of irony, and even though
    disheveled,
in body if not spirit, like our man in question, prepare
catholicons for manifold ills, from common nectars,
common nerves; from milk-tripods, pebble-blue, the
    amphibian
middle way opening out between the sea and cliffs; and
    from
all vined cliffs the beautiful and lovely wreaths the bodies
bend themselves into as laurel crowns for circling the
    brows
of champions. It's strange to think that we have spent

so much time around or near each other, like the wooden
men that trees were when they peopled a lonely earth—
two giant . . . foes? These handwritten notes are illegible.
Let's just say two giant foes in front of the gates of the
      alienating sea
that we are always being sent back to. Each puzzling
      sentiment
derives from some experience of some kind—one can
      only hope
the right kind; and one can only hope that there will be
a loving hand held to the nape of your neck, an affidavit
of delight, unfeigned, or unsigned, and so unsent, thus
unanswered, but found someday on marbled paper in
      a book
with An-Jing endsheets, a book about navigating by
      the stars.

THE BLOOMING OF SIGNIFICANCE

Whenas in silks the Department of Reviews
and Rebukes sends you its assessments
of your late performance, implex
with invective as a stick bug in a grass ball,
and unlike the false tangents of the dream dialectic
at play beneath the surface stream,
these stun us with an aptitude for pointed
shadows, fanciful descriptions and polyphonic
narrative, the prayer book's rainbow-colored text—
turn the page of light to the blinding
sonnet addressed to Cyriack Skinner.

It will be through a dismal series
of sureties and half-sensed, fleeting
premonitions, tender and light
and blossoming among the apparitions,
through notional prospects, the uninhibited
wind, that we will fall back upon ourselves,
upon what seemed like meager resources

but which now seems a quenching plenitude.
There was a jewel once paragon in you:
no flaw nor cloud, nor ice, dark facet,
but as a beam to the hunger, a house
to the grain; as beacon to shipwright,
the interceding walls of empty cantons
in front of the glittering sea—in that simple moment
you turned the page of light to the blinding
sonnet addressed to Cyriack Skinner,
you made a gesture almost narcissistic,
but innocently so, and slipped off
into the so-called stream of consciousness,
learning how to set all clocks by the water clock,
a series of water-beads on the marble sphere,
the "marble sphere of consciousness," which is
a real sphere, sitting motionless beside
the water clock of consciousness,
which is an actual clock, which is one more example
of the kind of creature that you wish to be,
so young and O, how that glittering taketh me,
toiling away under the stars at being so,
electuaries of herbs, roots, flowers, and seeds

dried in a gentle fire, just distant enough

from those with spleen enough

to carry you off beyond summer, beyond

your short and beautiful time on Earth

that is, on second thought, better than no time at all.

THE NEW ATLANTIS

These were the anonymous lands that you called home,
because they needed to be called something, if only for
    a moment.
And between this land and the anger of its logic, its
    corridors,
its blue and yellow papers doctrinaire, you moved
among those other aforementioned: skylarks singing
of the green flame and its likeness to the sea,
(the sea alive and purified of salt), the dream of utopian
    parity,
a kind of government to be wished for, not effected—
even dreaded in that unlikely circumstance: the City
of the Sun, the New Atlantis, the Anti-Cosmopolita,
its mentalities, much like its glittering towers, falling
through cascading levels of redundancy.

Do you think that children are raindrops? Or vice versa?
You who have slept in a bright ball of fog, one shaped
like a yellow apple streaked with blue and mottled green,
one hard, gray-green leaf still hanging from the stem—

let the rain fall down on us, here on Earth together
as if (as always) for the last time
before they bring down the retributory cudgel,
for even through all contests, contractions, and
    indictments,
through the clock-like spleen and wheels, racks, and
    brazen bulls,
harpies and catchpoles, wasps, mulcts, and jointures,
so pleasant it is to fall asleep beside you to the sound
    of waves:
but so, too, to go through the long night, sleepless,
and listen to the sound of waves.

COMMON MISNOMERS

The Mother of Pearl is the inner layer
of several sorts of shells. It is not the mother
of pearls as the name might seem to indicate,
but in some cases the matrix of the pearl.
It is a misnomer: as is the frontispiece,
mosaic gold, and the foxglove—as is honey soap,
Japan lacquer, and salt of lemon. You
were bending the truth, however gently, when you claimed
that this was yet another déjà vu, that you had looked
into a forest of bees identical to this one,
then charged ahead on the Green Man's Path,
but then ended up, as usual, among
strangers and solicitors—the sleeper cell
was just a bunch of sleepers, held lovingly
in one another's arms in an enchanted chamber
strewn with the bright green fragments of a giant insect.
If stones could grow grass, grass could perhaps give birth
to men, men to beasts and so on, there would then appear
some strange new kind of symbolism, one more akin
to your way of looking at objects,

where all things become themselves, but more so,
or at least your way of thinking things over,
yawning as they tumble by in the stream,
objects, box-like, unwieldy as box kites.
Here is some biographical information:
Nimbus clouds; lunar caustic; storms
floating in above the petrified forest—
then a burst of cedar waxwings, gray
and pale-yellow. Furthermore, I earned
an F in Trigonometry. I ate windowpane,
tried boiled cactus for hallucinations, and minute stems
accomplished the miracle of sudden blossoming
in bewildering solutions of grapes and eels
and deep forest truffles, and I was served
burnt applewood soaked in sweetened brine.
I slept in class, and slept so deeply that I dreamed.
And my friend Wayne wrote a comic book about it while
    I slept.
And in this book, the Buddha stood tall
in front of the suburban temple for Laotian immigrants,
and Wayne, you had me saying, faithful to the thing
that I had told you while I dreamed, that he
"looked taller when angered, taller than a blade of grass."

And we played the game called Stratagem of Interlocking
    Rings,
which always seemed to end in stalemate—
These are some among the common misnomers.

CLOUD IRIDESCENCE

Oiled paper nailed across storm windows.
A jelly cupboard made of yellow poplar.
Oil drums and corrugated metal: these
are the brightly colored flags of the originary nation.

And when I was a child of that nation,
in that nation, living in the geometric
buildings in the city of that nation,
the trucks drove past those structures
on a wide avenue lined with dark monuments
and statues of carnelian transparency,
bringing manganese to factories, and cobalt,
zinc for imparting brilliancy to pyrotechnics,
and great cubes of aluminum flashing in the sun.

Balloons were drifting over the world at dawn,
air balloons, airships, weather gauges made
of weightless silver foil, children's balloons,
globes of shimmering thought, clouds, gases,
large golden tufted spores. And down below,

the people lived their lives as ever, the misfits,
the star-crossed, the wooden proletariat,
and those just surviving off the oddments.
Like the astronomers you lived among during
your time on Earth, you too were prescient:
and it would be a typical cold and brilliant day
in yellowing silver grasses, free-wanderers
finding equilibrium, green and fierce
in the cloud of alternatives, airborne and haunted,
winged men. Some come to their senses
to find themselves safe, yet strangely so,
in the experimental caverns and the crystal cells
of emerald men. Others seem to drift in silence
toward a planet ringed by violet clouds—
but they are merely seeing summer through the doorway.

BOTANICAL GARDENS

Mechanical aldermen, celebrants and all good people:
The New Year cannons are booming—the cannons
of peace. They are booming over the garden and the city
of towers and spires rising over it. Giant orchids
are looming gently over the honey-colored gables,
the sloping rooftops made of berries, gnarled branches
twining over the brown facades. Giant wet ferns
lean against the side of Guyon-Lake-Tysen House,
blue lettuces flank the doors, large enough
for a circus strongman to hide in. See this house,
here on Eightysomething Street, roof of rough
bark, delicate red holly and minute pink flowers
almost hiding the doorway? This is where Edgar
Allan Poe wrote "The Oblong Box," and the story
about the chess-playing android. And here
is Pieter Claesen Wyckoff House, its roof of moss
and its mushroom chimney under the trestles
of a suspension bridge woven from sticks and twigs.
A yellow salt train passes. Bamboo sways
in the sky. You can lift a glowing yellow

fungus with both hands to reveal the doorway to the home
of Washington Irving. A second-floor window
glows softly: he's writing up there, pausing now and again
to bite his pencil and look out over the sail-like leaves
and the pointed houses built into the gorges.
The jasmine gardenia shadows the Astro-View Towers.
The Tent of Tomorrow, built for the World's Fair,
is crowned by a rattling seedpod and a pinecone.
A mansion, having risen once more
after an untimely demolition, looms, elevated
on a moss-covered stump. We have lived long enough
to see this. And you were one more train-spotter,
in a shirt besprent with seed pearls and diamonds small as
    raindrops
like Herman Melville struck by a refreshing blast of
    seaspray:
who offers you a bagel sprinkled with sea salt, berries,
and golden flax: an "everything bagel."

LETTER TO A FRIEND

It was at the New Year's celebration that we attempted to
   illuminate a cube of sugar
by small electrical explosion; to cause a stone to be in
   perpetual motion;
to break a stone with a blow of the fist, or with a
   "mercurial mallet";
to read the inscriptions on medals or roses in the dark
   with river spectacles;
to receive a shock of blue sparks from a cat or a number
   of household objects at once—
We were wondering, as well, what it meant to listen, and
   we did so simply by listening:
to the sounds of waves, which seemed to be the sound of
   listening itself.
And I thought you'd be excited that the leaves were
   flying before the closed doors,
aloft in the ambulant chamber from which you heard the
   opera, distant, and the shadows falling across the hills;
and the presiding sun, the President of Sunlight, seeming
   to gently command

———

that now was the time for hallucinations, and perhaps the
    mildest ever, mild as sunlight.
And yes: we were playing the Word Game as well—the
    game where we revealed the erstwhile secrets of who
    we were or who we had become,
not by saying anything about ourselves, but only saying
    the words themselves.
It was laying down tiles to form ideas, cold as Orion's
    Belt, as amaranth cutters,
if not significant then glittering like millions of dots of
    light and shadow scattered through branches:
this was the promise: that whatever to you I came bearing
    was merely a stand-in for something we both can agree
    was the dilemma the promise suggested:
they are very close to you; as close as anything that you
    might lay your eyes on, even lesser things, blue-violet,
the minute rain, diversions involving blue fire in each
    echoing room,
of fetishes carved out of wooden (pine, alder, cypress,
    mahogany) piston-like objects,
the small green and rounded soapstone fetishes, the
    ones "for luck," not hope, the ones for hope, not
    forgetting,

while down in the narrow precincts the color guard roam
    aimlessly having
spotted a toy-like yellow rocket on a tripod in the grass,
    giving them comfort,
as by reconcilers of a dilemma, always hopeful that
    accounts that can only be settled by accountants
    might be reconciled nonetheless,
and with the least possible public shaming, facile, among
    the tables set at dusk with giant water-pipes and
    peach tobacco,
the typical fluent concourse of the apiaries, the ill-used
    treasure
never to be summoned back after rejection and waste,
    the bottles broken hives, carburetors strewn in broken
    grass,
and still the menace that is also what seems the thing
    most worthy of living for,
though time was the Great Determiner, the Great
    Delimiter,
the Great and Unsure Man, and you were a word, in a
    role-playing game
in which you played the role of words.

THE MENTAL IMAGE

Corrugated steel domes red with oxidation
set in the winter weeds and crumbling snow.
Poems once had mental images, like these.
But they also overlaid a light-blue
or soft-rose transparency of ideation,
not like the maelstrom of bees
nor a glove on the hand of the huntress,
but a gentle adumbration of the same
maelstrom, a bodying forth
of the gemstone in the fable. The Law
is the law, even in the poem, even now—
though it is even larger now, as law,
and easier to go unrecognized as such,
and exact in the letter, but more exact
in spirit, and even more illuminated
in the letter.

THE STRANGE LIVES OF OTHERS

Cities were moving slowly over the land.
Stationary cities glittered in the sun.
What do you think of millions of rooms
with millions of people living their lives
inside them, people you will never know?
Some preening the coal-black wings
of paper planes to flick from windows, others
resting under soft globes of light, or chandeliers
of tangled crystal branches, having
sworn allegiance to the careworn ashplant
giant against the gnarled wall. Some
can see the park from their windows,
the needle-like towers behind the park, and over
the towers the sea and its towers, cities
honeycombed in gold; roaming cities.

In a Chinese room they are painting red leaves
on calico fustian with bamboo pens.
Sea widows walk the terraces along the gables,
patient and watchful. Meteors flare

against the sky, and over mahogany stairways
the portraits of ancestors in dark and angular
frocks are darkening the walls, one named
Oglala Violet Louise.

                    You've invented
the name for someone you will never know.
It is the orchestration you have trained for,
and then reimagined, outside Etruscan theaters
where still other strangers undergo their metamorphosis
into flames and yellow branches, their
transformation into friends, and friends still stranger:
then the winged men drifting down from the sky
in wide, slow circles.

THE CIGARIST

Pete Delaney smoking a cigar:
thoughtful in the courtyard, retired
repairer of steam-pipes, pugilist
at rest. Orange and amber smoke,
golden-gray and green, violet
and amber. Either/or. Either/or—
He is trying to decide. The crystal
rooftop and its cornice, greening
in the light shining on the cliffs:
it is neither here nor there—or it is here and there.
Pete Delaney walking over interlocking stones,
the common gray mosaic, puffing
his Dominican cigar, brown leaves, ragged
leaves redolent of boxwood. Either
it was equinox or solstice, both here
and in the capital, the shadows under
flaking tilted fountains in hidden patios
in Santo Domingo, green or yellow-green
or light green-yellow. This smoke
shadowed forth your calculations, Pete

Delaney, commonest of red-glass reliquaries
displaying Ming, aloft, for kindred spirits.
What can the sunrise of an idea
bring to light, if the sunrise shines
with winter light, far from these your
speculations? The day is bright.
Winter has come to an end. Spring
is nearer than it was in December,
and all things patrician in their ease of bearing
now grown beyond the ice's
self-annihilating glare. The snip
of round scissors is decisive,
Pete Delaney, the widower's turnip
one among the artisanal pleasures.
It is time for the taking of drastic measures,
for deciding what you can and cannot know.
He stubbed out his cigar
in an old and dirty clump of snow.

WHY DISTANT OBJECTS PLEASE

A wind-driven machine constructed
of myriad delicate sticks arranged
in an implex trestlework
of struts and quills and dowels
walked elegantly across the beach
on its hundreds of slender appendages,
two winglike sails revolving on its back.
If music is the universal language
then it is speaking to us silently
with a mantis-like telepathy. Let us
turn from it (though not away)
with superhuman equipoise,
and otherworldly grace, toward the sea.
Then let us make an observation
on some object whose attributes depend
on something hidden, and which are changing
imperceptibly—something other
than what is gathered up by the memory
and stored for later. These
are the giant clocks the sea waves made

when the smallest and nearest to the shore
were crossed by the shadow of Edward Shovelboard,
scattering the light around them,
trilling with obliterations, littered
with obliteratives that had washed in over the rocks,
the eyeliner pencils, the yellow plastic jugs
for cooking-oil, the empty vodka bottles
and the bleached-out labels on the weed-killer canisters.
Over there near the dunes, and some distance
from these signs of human habitation, two human beings
are sitting in the light of the benign sun,
watching a confluence of forces
come together to produce a sunset.

VOYAGES

You were playing the shell game
over near the shining vases
of smoky gray glass, then fell asleep
by the ritual flame, the ground
sprouting into golden wheat and barley
in the rain. The slim bottle seemed to smile
as the rays of light passed through it . . .
something interesting was happening
in the physical universe beside us.

And then I went traveling, and left you,
and set out for destinations far away
with ten sail on the good ship *The Swallow*,
with men of every faculty: Shipwrights
and Masons, Carpenters, Smithes, and such like,
requisite to such an action, and Minerall Men
and Refiners, passing near the Hebrides, Hesperides,
taking in apples and melons and strolling there
among strange fruit shops and a variety
of other objects. And I was away for years.

And every now and again, I would sink
into a Monstrous slumber among the cherry-gardens
in the lee of the turreted buildings on the grounds.
And I would dream of you.

And on my return trip home, I passed above
the Country of Common Work and the yellow beasts
that were guarding it; and over Mount Summer
and Mount Brilliant; and bamboo forests
rising high into the clouds and all the purple stones
of cities and the Valley of Enameled Bastions.

And when I landed, you were waiting at the airport
in a blue car, you were naked underneath a long coat,
which you opened slightly with one hand as we crossed
the bridge, exposing your breasts, and we stopped then
at a motel at the city's dark outskirts, where we found
our room prepared for us, and I knelt beside the bed
while you disappeared for a moment,
and then came back dressed as a nurse; and then
you disappeared a second time and returned
in the habit of a nun; and you went away and came back
dressed as the chief of police, and next as Master

and Commander, and next as a huntress, then
a quarryman, and then a thief. And then
it was my turn: and I will not tell you all the things
that I pretended to be, the things we did
and pretended to do. Only that we
debased ourselves, abject and beautiful,
and then dressed as ourselves; and after a while,
we lay naked by the window, smoking,
just watching the airplanes flying off into the sky.

EDDIE DESIRÉE LOVES AURORA BAKER

Eddie Desirée loves Aurora Baker.
And Russo loves a girl named Opal Waive.
Eddie was a locker-room lawyer, a bum-paper
artist and a cardsharp, a cigar store
philosopher and a three-card monte hustler.
Russo was a cabbage hat, a pawnbroker,
a virtuoso of the "Chinese saxophone."
But on this day they were in the open air,
on the ferry chugging past Lady Liberty,
the great Metallic Lady, the monolithic
woman of greened bronze, standing
in the chilly waters of the harbor, diademed,
her headgear of radiating spikes, acid green,
there before the rank on rank of buildings
in the City Rampant and its lions sleeping,
countercouchant, before libraries and theaters,
and domes; and there, there on the ocean
in the setting sun, on the same waves
underneath which braver men than they were sleeping,
there where the reach of a dark armistice ended

———

and something undefined began—
there on a boat named *Mary Murray*
late riveted and fired in the Bethlehem Steel yards,
those two kindred spirits loved the smokestacks
and the coral-golden smoke, and Eddie Desirée
loves Aurora Baker of Schenectady, New York;
and Russo loves a girl named Opal Waive.

THE TOPOGRAPHY OF THE MOON

They will go back to the land. To Mother Earth
and her brothers, her angry uncles and her long-lost
    sisters,
back to the land like Crusoe, washed ashore,
watching grapes shrivel in the sun.
This is where the wheel is broken at the cistern
and the weeds of dandelion rise to over six feet tall,
their star-shaped heads not yet in blossom.
They know they are estranged from something
to which they somehow belonged. In consequence
they will go forth, the people of these tenements: he
who improvises tools to open waterworks; the hoarders
and the unofficial mayors and the aldermen;
those who tend feral cats in the trash-strewn gorges;
the vendors of radishes and the vendors of green ice;
keepers of the secret aviary; the men who repair
the gear-work of elevators, returning home
in grass-green uniforms, drunk and half asleep
under a system of stars called Swan;
smokers of cigars flavored with lavender;

those destroyed by radiance for cancers;
he that guides the giant freighters into port
or inspects a crate of green plantains for stinging
insects; the soldier envisioning a blue flare;
she who willingly sends her child
through the viridescent grass to granite headlands;
those who observe the breeding habits of a thrush
through concave and cylinder glasses in the verdant
ruined theater; who tend the salt-fires
made from dried kelp gathered from the sea at high tide;
who cultivate the blue vervain and sweet alyssum;
the lathemen and workers of an iron beam,
or who lays down a layer of coal-tar and slag;
the sellers of fireworks and amaryllis
or he who poaches stingray from the sea;
who writes a synopsis of the first partition;
who studies the peach-colored glaze on ancient crockery
or smokes mint tobacco while cutting the street with a
    diamond saw;
he who polishes an obelisk or polishes the windows
of a green prismatic tower. The glass and plaster rubble
hauled by the barge *Buchanan Reverence* flows into the
    sun

toward autumn. And though we begin in the middle of
     things,
so do they, and everything else, for that matter.
The concrete structures of the state's planned housing
empty out, people walk into the sun to congregate
on green space, among the colonies of lucid moss,
the swarms of bees, and theories and beliefs
begin to break apart to be replaced by something else:
like love, it is easy to say what it is not,
nearly impossible to say what it is.
They will go back to the land, to the moon, where all
     things forgotten
have been scattered among the strange sunflowers
near the house of the Interpreter, in the company
of shining ones, and one another.

SIX RECORDS OF A FLOATING LIFE

Every man is best known to himself. Every man hath
his proper gift. Every man in his way. Every man must
    bear
his own burden. Every man may not wear a furred hood.
And every man mend one, and all shall be mended. Every
    man.

Every man's censure first is molded in his nature. Every
man must row with such oars as he has. Every man has a
    fool
in his sleeve; is the architect of day. Every man spinneth
webs beside which weeds grow apace. Every man on a
    bridge

made of rag and glass is born, and some in a comet
year, some in a year of wonders, some steeped in marl for
    widows,
some beneath a mushroom, some beneath the vulcan
    furnace,
some in a garden pink-tinged with bees and amaryllis near
    an ornamental

---

fountain, some near the sea. This is where he can be
    everything at once,
where the rose of Sharon is narcissus, narcissus rose of
    Sharon
"the nearer they dwell to the waterside," which is why
    you opened the window,
and now lie here abed, unsleeping, a slim frond waving
    in a gentle wind.

AND WHAT OF Z?

I've been a reader nearly all my life, ever since before I could speak, even: I have been reading, been read to . . . have run across the Little Bs in their teeming countlessness, been subject to the purling forth of Big C, of Little D scattering from great purging fans, of myriad and shining E bending down the boughs, in harvest home, in seeding, in bringing forth, in the ripening purple grapes of wine trailing down from Wednesday's briar. And what of supernumerary G? And what of Z?

Now, Great A comes, rising up as if from nowhere. And now, O little boy, your small bed breaks into blossom. The Iron Age begins its slow decline. Beyond the fields and on the waters we can see the sunrise-colored sails on the lacquered boats of Q.

THE RESPONDERS

Men with mustaches are running toward
the tower, old-fashioned men in fireproof
coats, with grappling hooks and axes,
masked and hooded, their heads
like nightingales in metal helmets.
Aren't they like fathers
of a certain generation, stoic
and unspeaking in the thunder and rain,
resigned to be exhausted, uninterpreted,
wandering through gold-colored
smoke into the night?
These are such that daughters never told
their secrets to. They are not the clever
men who will live, bolts of brightly colored
cloth unspooling. They are postdiluvian
giants, they are animists, they spark life
there on the ramparts of the city dark
and tenebrous, their dark or blond or bronze
mustaches combed out into flaming points.

We were reading the decorative tiles
on our visit to the House of Life,
its seemingly sequential rooms, stairways
leading past an alabaster curio,
toward the upper stories where the mothers
who outlive their children were residing.
And the faces of the children
are those of grown men on the cameos
on the rocks around the water-features
in the garden far below, rainbow-tinged,
inlaid in the stone with mother-of-pearl.
These women have no need to tell their stories:
they know that someday you will know them, too.

ALBANY

There they were at sunset
standing on the parapet
that overlooked the river,
rolling (and smoking)
cigarettes, and watching
the sun go down behind
New Jersey. They were three:
an erstwhile preacher; a wino
of the garden variety; an
impersonator of Elvis; they
gathered there each evening
around the preacher's radio
and revolved the mysteries
of war and peace among them,
economies, conspiracies, all
subjects of prevaricators.
Barges were flowing down the river
from capital cities, nocturnal
Hong Kongs and Albanys upstate
where monuments paid tribute

to wheat and grapes, steel
and mariners and civil engineers,
where beehives and their keepers
were carved into the granite
walls of looming clock towers.
And where were they going?
That was a matter for further
consideration (the pastor
cracked open another can of beer).
In the public garden behind them:
Some silkworms sleeping on mulberry leaves;
a woman, standing tall, observing
sunset on the pathway;
an Attic vase beneath the stars.

MAY I JOIN THE CHOIR INVISIBLE

In Lexington Charles (Walter) Faxon
used to find warblers in the fall
startling them from beds of jewelweed.
The evening was the playtime for the thrush
and their allies, and all twilight-loving
birds were emerging from concealing shadows.
Darkness enveloped the woods:
all was calm for the wanderer.
For a time peace seemed to prevail.
A great clock ticked. The rough golden hedges,
the subterminal blackish bands on plumage
read like a clear though secretive book.
As if sent to him alone to apprehend
the felicities of evening, a bunch of grapes
is unwrapped from walnut-colored paper,
and one apple, marbled with hallucinations,
signals the way through the boundless
though ascertainable forest.

PRODIGIES

The child prodigy was a prodigy
beyond description—a colossus,
a titan, saturnine, prodigious
in stature, an Elgin marble.
His wig stood tall atop his head
as if a small person, perhaps
a smaller, younger child prodigy,
were standing there hidden cleverly
inside it. And one might say that one
yet still smaller lived inside this one.
He was normal in some ways:
his mother loved him, his father
took him to task but loved him, too,
as the sky lit up in the light
of the comet, or darkened in the dark
of the eclipse. The child prodigy
composed an opera involving love
and magic, evil, honor and treachery,
ice-like men, visible through vine-leaves,
and how the dead took revenge

against the universe for vastness;
and he composed this opera
mentally amid the laurel trees
in the aspen forest, or among the leaning
moss-covered houses of ghost cities.
And do you remember how, while he played
the harpsichord for grown-ups
in his golden ringlets, the ruffles
from his silk sleeves dangling down,
we walked along the seaside
at dawn near the Rainbow Alfoxden
where the saline meadowlark nested
and the indigo bunting would never
be aware of the meaning of her song?
Storm clouds had something to say
to us—just not something very
significant. Under chandeliers
we are small for a very short time,
growing like grass at the tall door.

MY NAME IS DUSTIN HEMP

My name is Dustin Hemp.
Do you recall the famous words
of Danton? "Be sure to show the mob
my head"? Dustin Hemp too
is merely a forked radish, a mandrake
root with beard, a butternut squash with brains.
Torquato Tasso wrote *Jerusalem Delivered*
in the 1570s. It is thousands of pages long
and tells the story of Godfrey
and his crusaders. Dustin Hemp
has not read *Jerusalem Delivered*. Ariosto wrote
Orlando furioso, an epic in forty-six cantos
about the siege of Paris by Agramante the Moor.
The anachronisms in the poem are most marvelous.
And yet, strange to say, Dustin Hemp
has not read the *Furioso*. What about Gower's
Confessio Amantis? What about Wolfram's
Wilhelm? Dustin Hemp has not read 'em.
And Pietro Bembo's *Canzoniere*?
Let alone read, it was too thick to carry.

Add this to your list of grievances:
Dustin Hemp has not read the new translation
of the Ramayana, national epic of India,
nor has he read the New Selected Wallace Stevens,
nor the Sanskrit epilogue appended thereunto,
nor Helen Vendler's lemon-scented acrostics
written on consecutive vanilla prisms.
He has not read the Hexaglot Bible,
the Bug Bible, the Breeches Bible,
the Idle Bible, the Vinegar Bible,
the Place-Makers' Bible, or the Clog Almanac.
He has not read the closet dramas
of Alexander, Earl of Stirling, nor his
poem sequence *Aurora*. He has not reclined
upon Cowper's couch, nor wandered in Breton's
Arbor of Amorous Devices, nor maneuvered
through the scintillating thorns of Gayatri Spivak's
translation of Derrida's *Of Grammatology*.
Mr. Hemp, your library is a panoply
of iridescent darkness. Now
as you rest beneath the willow
lay the book down beside your pillow
and forget yourself.

EVERYBODY ELSE

This is one hand's flowing blue script
on a page set aside for later. Are you just
one small person sleeping in the billows of your life
like everybody else? Observe the sunset
on the green prison turrets
downriver from the new mall full of vacant stores
of this provincial town, its feral cats and hoarders,
its decorative weaponry trained on the perplexed
and opposite shore where every crooked house
is cobbled together from adages and junk;
chunks of yellow ice and tripods; volts and wire;
cylinders, fuses, paste, and fire.
The circumfluent waters by the planing mill are violet—
they are the waters of the city, and the waters of the sky.
And in one of that town's shops that sells antiques
the five-year diary of Florence Mangham is propped
between Chinese plate and a Civil War saber:
page after page of yellowed entries in a flowing hand
in deep blue ink: "February 21, 1957:
Busy all the a.m.; busy all the whole day . . ."

CITIES AT DAWN

As soon as you think
you are writing a poem,
or should be, you
turn to something else,
let it issue its commands
when you rail in
what we all agree
will be, and near. Then
it is the Sayer's Day,
and winged apples wave
in the sea-waves.

★

Purple apples snapping
under hailstones
are as logical
and cavernous as summer;
and the green
unfinished apples
blink as flames

on the ends of tapers
and sleep. And the sleeping
pods in the Empire
State Building are near
completion, so you may
nap there soon
while it rains in the breaking
dawn.

★

The specificity beyond
reason is black.
The pink tennis
courts, the pink sky
above the larches
around the tennis
courts at disk.
At (rather) dusk.

★

All the broken birds
are in the weird green gables
simply readying themselves

to beam you with their jetting
through the glassine tower-wires
high above the swollen
foxgloves.

★

White apples lopped off
twisted branches
by harvesters, with tenterhooks
sharp as shears for manzanita;
white apples
have in wild milkweed
surely lain.

★

Pinetum after rain.
Law firm at night.
Sparkling cones.
Bloated pods.

★

Walked . . . walking . . .
waking . . . okay—walking

across the Great Lawn
on rainy afternoon;
blue needles bending
down, beading down; blue
needles sharpened
by raindrops in the wet
pinetum: Great Lens.

★

Did you recognize me
when I was playing the part
of your past come back
as a stranger?
And I was up
in a haunted turret
among the waving green
cresses and the ivies
dawn was roaring down with.

★

Outside, a book in a light-green jacket
sprang up
like a hat out of ice plant:

the diaries of Dorothy Wordsworth.
March 20, 1802, was a glorious day.

★

"As the clock drips"?
Oh, a water clock.
I was learning to tell time
by the dew clock.
I was longing to be there
early, to meet you.
Yellow-green peelings fluttered down
from the tall sycamores.
It was six o'clock on the frosted mansard.
It seems I wrote a lowercase *y*—
I turned my head, and its tail
started growing downward,
like a root, or something
pronging, penetrating, probing
down beneath its blue line.
Let's wrap up: the red sunflowers
are running through the garden, singing.

★

83

Better than the propaganda
of these things I think
should be said:
Nail a tin sheet
with a ball-peen hammer
over the words, hiding them
forever with a shiny thing.

⋆

And a great deal
of mountain sky
has been untouched, finally;
your sentences need not all
be axiomatic;
so just, then, sink
to your knees, then,
in grass, in-grass,
tall grass.

⋆

Sequence of red windows
glassing in the pears
in the light they'd been wanting

to be seen by:
sun-stories, gambrels,
the chapel's dark onset.

★

I wish I could say something comforting to you
that would wash over you like rain
and then disappear, and it would be me
and this wish to affect you, who need
nothing from me, that would disappear,
a beet with a yellowish root in the ground.
I like the Korean dictionary.

★

A. canceled his trip to tradeshow
in Shanghai, China, for
tentacles, its lonely glories
glowing in rye fields
and many towers tall
as a lesson in statistics' lift
of honeybees against you.

★

A several-pronged cloud
was jutting out across
the stratosphere and Fuji,
and forming a complete
person, alive with failings,
which is a ghost shaking
hands with your glories,
which is a ghost. So
the evergreens, over
and ever there,
dripping morning rain,
make you seem more
alive in your life.

★

Let's arrange to have water
with our tea.
Then stone limes,
then lozenges.
And it's pristine
to be rising, or just
awake.

★

———

Be calm sometimes
in the winter, when it's snowing
and the boats are lost,
the long, slow boats
in the giant river.

★

Alone in pinetum.
Chains on empty swingsets
clanging.
Mountain flags.

★

Children playing
in the angled green shadows
of the town houses.

★

The square root
of an oak
is imaginary.
We are imaginary
and amazing, touching,

finally, one another
fiercely, with no call
to sleep in a giant
wakefulness.

★

Plate glass, anthems,
sides, placeholders,
gains and losses . . .
scent of peach rain
on yellow notebook.
White sails on wide
river, radical, free.

★

The map of Persia was small
enough to funnel rain into a footprint
on the floodplain.

★

Now something is happening to you—
just pretend you're referring to the tide.

*

Then cool rays
where there are red
butterflies,
mountains turned
against you.

*

Fragrant, mythic
flowers, fragmenting
points and adjustments
breaking through
watery air.

*

Over the shoulder
of a man the building
startled us with
sunrise beside and behind
it. Let's be
like it, or what
we think it is.

———

What it should be
as us in seeing it
(is us seeing it).

★

The skylights are wide
open, exposing rows
of white beams
and whiter, and cool
white beams that lift
the panes of glass
skyward.

★

We waded out into the brown
water of the square lake—
is it man
made? Is a square man
made? Dozens
of white geese floated
on the water out beyond the buoys.

★

What you said you saw
was green tiles on the boulevard
and vapor trails as greens go
to their gains
on skyways
to their jade gems
and sea foam.

★

Lens of spectacle
drops into the water
with a plop
and the sharp leaves
blunt against the sky.

★

Stark, inarguable logic
leads to bombs
and the clocks exposed
atop the old
New York Times
headquarters.

★

Partial view of limekilns
in the mountains of Germany;
stacks of brown felt
satisfy the statistician
on the floor
of the former staple factory.

★

I could see only one A
large on the back cover
of the book that he
was carrying, the old
man. But it was such
an A I thought that I
had shared, been part of,
read, and spoken of,
that we had been there,
I and that old man.
The A sparkled in the
purple-green raindrops
of sudden shower.

———

*

Men on smooth building-side
in yellow helmets lowered down
on scaffold and white ropes.
They sand down the wall
with powerful abrasives.
White puffs of chalk,
of residue, billow out.

*

Bran flour burns
into the reddish steeples.
Its simple tables
merely tremble
as the private men
slumber.

*

Turn the crank
and the yellow awning
stretches out on
bending silver arms
and yellows over buildings.

———

★

Great red birdfeeders
in the branches set
asway—it's cheap
to be reliant on music,
pliant, alive in trills.

★

The gas cooler
of the cokery
is striated by iron
trellises, silver chutes,
and stairwells wind
around it; the white
cylinders of cement trucks
spin, strawberries spin.

★

An excruciatingly dense
plum sphere
has formed
in the branches of a wet tree.

★

The song, as it
came to be known,
was what I saw fall
down, in midsleep,
thinking it was me, or that
it should have been,
or that once reckoned,
would add up to being
me. But it was shocking
to be so frozen
into waking again after
a time, and I there
came to know only
something outward tho appealing
of an outside moment.

★

You could only see the sun once
from the district mountains
light on the apple barley
colder to refresh us
quick from pleasant slumber.

———

*

You've rested with opinions
red as apple skins
. or gold trimming
the border of the flags
waving over underrepresented
places.

*

Ask then what the sphere
suggested with its plum
finish purple
and the striated hedges
of the hawthorn and
the manzanita seemingly
aflame in its serrations.

*

This blue and red-jacketed
retelling of the Ramayana
is remaindered, marked down
to nine ninety-eight.

———

Brand-new people
dot the populace
always, shadows
pointing underneath
the spires of the hospital.

★

Silkworms spin
in rattling appalling
leaves appealing
threads for neckties,
strands for a shy girl's
dew-dotted sandals.

★

The yellow-green currants,
eye-like, shining,
seem to see you.

★

In Randers, major
manufacturing and trade center
north-northwest of Århus

on the Jutland peninsula
of Denmark, the winding
towers and the furnaces stand too,
thirteen dandelion stems
stand too, and tall,
slenderer as they near the sky.

★

The snowdrifts
still loft up
along the runners
of the locomotives
and coils heat up
a kettle of red water
for the rusty tea
you have been given.

★

Ripplewood Holdings
was the name of the concern
that held plaudits
from announcers
on the waves

in high esteem
from fields to shipyards
where spun rivets
and aggression
were subject
to chemical change
and physical change, like
steam over acreage.

★

To bring off the string
of birds like light
successes over rooftops
the poem counts
to ten in the trees.

★

Small head of chef
in brown ink
in a sun
on a sugar packet
near the coffee
is, of course, idealized

as he gazes out at you
forever working at his task
to augment sweetness.

★

The winter rockets
and the watercresses
both of which
have large, sad leaves
that lie upon the ground
like turnip strands.

★

Could I see
from the Shanghai Brightness Factory
the toys shipped out
along the gem-clips?

★

Or the sweet, delicious,
tall tea glacier
melting in the sun.

★

Give one detail
about the iris.
It is very popular.
We will be writing
about them, and telling them
about themselves, that
cannot listen, but lift up
nonetheless, purple
toward the details.

★

Something was looking at me
through a grating
of plum foliage
and blinked its eyes.

★

Japanese train station
lunch book at dawn.
It's the delicate arrangement
of the sun and clouds
above the rail yard—
and the distant mountains.

———

WINDING TOWERS

In any shallow ravine along a train track,
anywhere in these United States, one can always find,
without fail, a discarded mattress slumped amid
the desiccated bracken. Why? It would seem that,
    sleep-wise,
we are an ambivalent nation. The sky is gray-green
above the monumental spiral-guided gas tanks, above
the gray stone breakers for basalt that slump uncertainly
amid debris, temples gone to sleep. And while you're
    reading
John Needham's history of China, turn to the part
on building stanchions for suspension bridges,
or the myriad towers of wind farms—
or the chapter on posterity, and how
it lengthens away from you through a haze,
gray and turning golden, of futurity.

Farmers and workers look out over glittering fields
and even as far as where the curve of the earth
becomes visible. Some will be transported

to some provincial prefecture,
made petty bureaucrats or pressed into service
on distant battlefields, or roused awake
on a shining green peninsula—the sea,
bathing their feet, cold as a chiming bell
in the wide, free air. "The Geography of Sea-Walls"
is just one chapter in that book, as is
"The Tract on Sacred Enclosures": a strange volume,
even among the strange things of the living forest,
the short-winged birds of passage,
the wheatears and the martins, that flow
into grottoes tangled in vines
and out again on their way to the sky.
You have taken its spirit to heart.
And though delivered in the dark similitude of a dream,
it opens like gates and passageways around you,
revealing an enormous realm of overtness.
The golden wheat and barley, so important
to men, appear in the distance, where all things meet.

MARVELL AND SHENSTONE/
SHENSTONE AND MARVELL

Mosque-like domes, water towers,
spires, turrets, masts, steeples,
gambrels, mansards; big piles
of gravel by the tan gravel-crushing
structure; whitened corncobs
strewn on the grass among
the bent cigarette butts; Andrew
Marvell, the Tree of Ideas
is glistening, the branches
are spectral, and the leaves,
even in this wind, are myriad.
The materials at your disposal,
William Shenstone, are elemental
and refractory. The apples, cool
and round, are wooden apples,
glass apples, metal apples;
wine is kept in one, and in the others
salt, nutmeg, rosewater, ink,

and an unidentified elixir. Andrew Marvell,
William Shenstone, the breeze
blows cool and strong. The sunset . . .
the sunset is peach-colored;
and it is . . . deepening.
The mystery is deepening
as it grows closer to you.

ACKNOWLEDGMENTS

Several fellow poets carefully read this book in manuscript and offered helpful feedback and encouragement: Tom King, Jeff Dolven, Cort Day, Randall Potts, and David Joel Friedman. Regan Good, Mark Levine, Kumi Yamashita, Brent Arnold, Emily Wilson, Erik Maahs, and Maria Diaz also offered their love, friendship, and encouragement during the years I was writing this book. My gratitude to Brian Young, whose poems showed the world-changing possibilities of the imagination. Thank you to my friends at Wave Books: Charlie Wright, Heidi Broadhead, Brittany Dennison, Joshua Beckman, my friend and editor Matthew Zapruder. Thank you, David Caligiuri at Two Hungry Rabbits and Jeff Clark at Quemadura.

Some of these poems or earlier versions of these poems first appeared: *Augury Books, The Winter Anthology, Better, Vondervotteimitis, Hinchas de Poesia,* and *Wag's Revue.* Thank you, Jenny Mueller and Brian Young, for publishing the chapbooks *Four Poems* and *The Mountains of Spring* through Polyphemus Press, in which several of the poems in *Cites at Dawn* first appeared.

I want to express my gratitude to the amazing poets—friends and kindred spirits all—of the Wallson Glass Seminars. And to my brothers and sisters in spirit, the dead poets: whose light, like that of stars long gone out, reaches us after traveling great distances through time and space, and glitters with living brilliance.

Hail fellowship—brief text, bright answering.

DAVID JOEL FRIEDMAN